GOOD HOUSEKEEPING

EATING ITALIAN

The essence—and beauty—of Italian cookery lies in its simplicity, so you need have no fear about tackling any of the recipes in this book. From pizzas, the classic convenience food, through pasta, easy and satisfying for speedy suppers, to veal and trout, perfect for special dinners for friends. They're all so delicious that your only problem will be in choosing where to start.

With the compliments of

COOKERY NOTES

Follow either metric or imperial measures for the recipes in this book as they are not inter-changeable. Sets of spoon measures are available in both metric and imperial size to give accurate measurement of small quantities. All spoon measures are level unless otherwise stated. When measuring milk we have used the exact conversion of 568 ml (1 pint).

* Size 2 eggs should be used except when otherwise stated.
† Granulated sugar is used unless otherwise stated.
● Plain flour is used unless otherwise stated.

OVEN TEMPERATURE CHART

°C	°F	Gas mark
110	225	$\frac{1}{4}$
130	250	$\frac{1}{2}$
140	275	1
150	300	2
170	325	3
180	350	4
190	375	5
200	400	6
220	425	7
230	450	8
240	475	9

KEY TO SYMBOLS

`1.00*` Indicates minimum preparation and cooking times in hours and minutes. They do not include prepared items in the list of ingredients; calculated times apply only to the method. An asterisk * indicates extra time should be allowed, so check the note below symbols.

⌂ Chef's hats indicate degree of difficulty of a recipe: no hat means it is straightforward; one hat slightly more complicated; two hats indicates that it is for more advanced cooks.

£ Indicates a recipe which is good value for money; £ £ indicates an expensive recipe. No £ sign indicates an inexpensive recipe.

✳ Indicates that a recipe will freeze. If there is no symbol, the recipe is unsuitable for freezing. An asterisk * indicates special freezer instructions so check the note immediately below the symbols.

`309 cals` Indicates calories per serving, including any suggestions (e.g. cream, to serve) given in the ingredients.

METRIC CONVERSION SCALE

LIQUID			SOLID		
Imperial	Exact conversion	Recommended ml	Imperial	Exact conversion	Recommended g
$\frac{1}{4}$ pint	142 ml	150 ml	1 oz	28.35 g	25 g
$\frac{1}{2}$ pint	284 ml	300 ml	2 oz	56.7 g	50 g
1 pint	568 ml	600 ml	4 oz	113.4 g	100 g
$1\frac{1}{2}$ pints	851 ml	900 ml	8 oz	226.8 g	225 g
$1\frac{3}{4}$ pints	992 ml	1 litre	12 oz	340.2 g	350 g
For quantities of $1\frac{3}{4}$ pints and over, litres and fractions of a litre have been used.			14 oz	397.0 g	400 g
			16 oz (1 lb)	453.6 g	450 g
			1 kilogram (kg) equals 2.2 lb.		

Illustrated on the cover: Four Seasons Pizza (page 24) and Pizza with Four Cheeses (page 25)

GOOD HOUSEKEEPING

EATING ITALIAN

Contents

STARTERS	4
PASTA, RICE AND GNOCCHI	12
PIZZAS	24
MAIN COURSES	30
VEGETABLE ACCOMPANIMENTS	44
SWEET THINGS	48
INDEX	63

PARMA HAM WITH MELON

PROSCIUTTO CON MELONE

| 0.20 | £ £ | 104 cals |

Serves 4

900 g (2 lb) Cantaloupe melon
8 thin slices of Parma ham
freshly ground black pepper

1 Cut the melon in half lengthways. Scoop out the seeds from the centre.

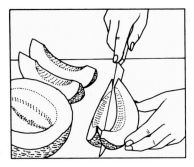

2 Cut each of the melon halves into four even-sized wedge shapes.

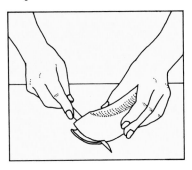

3 With a sharp, pointed knife and using a sawing action, separate the flesh from the skin, keeping it in position on the skin.

4 Cut the flesh across into bite-sized slices, then push each slice in opposite directions.

5 Carefully roll up each of the eight slices of Parma ham. Place two wedges of melon and two rolls of ham on each plate. Grind pepper over the ham before serving.

---- VARIATION ----

Instead of the melon, use fresh figs in season to make Prosciutto Con Fichi. Only use very fresh, ripe figs in peak condition. In Italy, figs are often served whole and unpeeled, but to help guests who are not used to eating figs as much as the Italians are, it is best to peel them first, then cut them in half. For four people, 8–12 figs is sufficient. Arrange them cut-side up on individual serving plates next to the Parma ham, which may or may not be rolled up, according to how you like it.

MARINATED MUSHROOM SALAD

INSALATA DI FUNGHI

0.10*	£	222 cals

* plus 2 hours marinating

Serves 4

90 ml (6 tbsp) olive oil

30 ml (2 tbsp) lemon juice

salt and freshly ground pepper

225 g (8 oz) firm button mushrooms

8 anchovy fillets, soaked in milk (optional)

30 ml (2 tbsp) chopped fresh parsley, to garnish

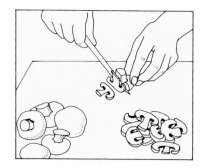

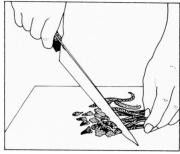

1 Make the dressing. In a medium bowl, mix together the olive oil, lemon juice and freshly ground pepper. (Do not add salt at this stage if you are using anchovies.)

2 Slice the mushrooms finely, then add to the dressing and mix well to coat evenly. Cover and leave to stand in a cool place for at least 2 hours.

3 Just before serving, chop the anchovy fillets, if using, and stir into the mushrooms. Check seasoning and garnish with the chopped parsley.

MOZZARELLA-STUFFED TOMATOES
POMODORI RIPIENI ALLA MOZZARELLA

| 0.40* | 491 cals |

* plus at least 2 hours chilling

Serves 4

4 large, firm tomatoes

salt and freshly ground pepper

50 g (2 oz) black olives

225 g (8 oz) Italian Mozzarella cheese, grated

1–2 garlic cloves, skinned and crushed

20 ml (4 tsp) chopped fresh basil or 10 ml (2 tsp) dried

135 ml (9 tbsp) olive oil

45 ml (3 tbsp) lemon juice

fresh basil sprigs, to garnish

3 Scoop out the insides of the tomatoes with a sharp-edged teaspoon. Sprinkle the insides with salt and stand the tomatoes cut side down to drain on absorbent kitchen paper.

4 Make the stuffing. Reserve four whole black olives, then stone and chop the remainder.

5 Put the Mozzarella in a bowl with the chopped olives, garlic and half the basil. Mix well to combine, then add salt and pepper to taste. (Add salt sparingly because olives tend to be salty.)

6 Place the tomatoes cut side up in a serving dish. Spoon the Mozzarella mixture into the tomatoes, dividing it equally between them. Replace the reserved tomato slices at an angle so that the Mozzarella filling is visible.

7 Whisk together the oil and lemon juice with the remaining basil and salt and pepper to taste. Pour over the tomatoes, then chill in the refrigerator for at least 2 hours, spooning the dressing over from time to time. Serve chilled, garnished with the reserved olives and the basil sprigs.

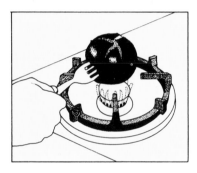

1 Skin the tomatoes. Pierce them one at a time in the stalk end with a fork or skewer and hold over a gas flame or under the grill. Turn the tomato constantly until the skin blisters and bursts, then leave until cool enough to handle. Peel off the skin with your fingers.

2 Cut a slice off the bottom (rounded end) of each tomato. Reserve the slices.

POMODORI RIPIENI ALLA MOZZARELLA

This recipe uses Italian Mozzarella cheese for its soft creamy texture which mixes smoothly with other ingredients. Italian Mozzarella is imported from Italy and also manufactured outside Italy by Italians living abroad—it can be easily identified by its waxed paper wrapping. The cheese inside is moist and fresh, often dripping with whey. Mozzarella made in Scotland or Denmark, which is a harder, waxy cheese, is not suitable for this recipe, although it can be used as a substitute for Mozzarella in recipes such as pizza where it is melted. The best substitute for the Mozzarella in this recipe would be Ricotta or a full-fat soft cheese or cream cheese.

SEAFOOD SALAD
INSALATA DI FRUTTI DI MARE

1.05* ⊟ £ £ 443 cals

* plus 2 hours chilling

Serves 6

1.1 litres (2 pints) fresh mussels, cleaned and cooked, with cooking liquor reserved

2.8 litres (5 pints) water

1 onion, skinned and roughly chopped

1 bay leaf

salt and freshly ground pepper

350 g (12 oz) squid, cleaned

350 g (12 oz) shelled scallops

350 g (12 oz) peeled prawns, thawed and thoroughly dried if frozen

1 small green pepper, cored, seeded and finely sliced into strips

1 small red pepper, cored, seeded and finely sliced into strips

1 carrot, peeled

150 ml (¼ pint) olive oil

60 ml (4 tbsp) lemon juice

30 ml (2 tbsp) capers

45 ml (3 tbsp) chopped fresh parsley

1 garlic clove, skinned and crushed

black olives, to garnish

1 In a large saucepan, mix together the cooking liquor from the mussels and 1.75 litres (3 pints) of the measured water. Add the onion, bay leaf and a pinch of salt and bring to the boil. Add the squid and simmer gently for 20 minutes or until tender.

2 Remove the squid from the cooking liquid in the pan and set aside.

3 Bring the liquid back to the boil, add the scallops and poach gently for 3 minutes. Remove the scallops from the liquid with a slotted spoon and set aside. (Reserve the fish liquid for making a fish soup.)

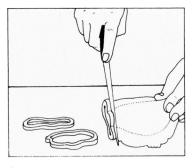

4 Using a sharp knife, cut the squid into rings approximately 1 cm (½ inch) wide.

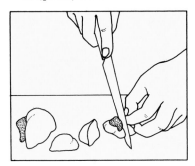

5 Cut the scallops into four, removing the tough muscle (found near the coral or roe).

6 Reserve a few mussels in their shells for the garnish. Remove the shells from the remaining mussels and put the mussels in a large serving bowl with the squid, prawns and scallops. Add the sliced peppers.

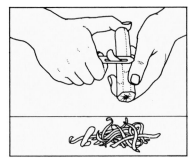

7 With a potato peeler, shred the carrot into ribbons and add this to the seafood.

8 Make the dressing. Mix together the oil, lemon juice, capers, parsley and garlic—with pepper to taste. Pour over the seafood. Mix lightly but thoroughly. Taste and add salt if necessary.

9 To serve. Chill for at least 2 hours and then serve garnished with black olives and the reserved mussels in shells.

INSALATA DI FRUTTI DI MARE
All the fish and shellfish specified in this recipe are available at most high-class fishmongers, but if you have difficulty finding one particular kind it isn't absolutely necessary to follow the recipe to the letter. Italian seafood salads vary enormously, depending on the time of year and the availability of fresh fish and shellfish—Italian cooks would far rather make a salad from one top-quality fish than a mixture of inferior ones. Freshness and quality are the keynotes with any Italian seafood dish, and this is worth bearing in mind when shopping—mussels, squid and scallops all have their own 'seasons', so it is worth checking with your fishmonger before buying.

HOT ANCHOVY DIP
BAGNA CAUDA

| 0.45 | 🥄 | 396 cals |

Serves 6

225 g (8 oz) asparagus, washed, trimmed and freshly cooked

3 globe artichokes, trimmed and freshly cooked

1 small cauliflower

1 large red pepper

1 large green pepper

4 carrots, peeled

6 celery sticks, trimmed

3 courgettes, trimmed

1 bunch radishes

150 ml ($\frac{1}{4}$ pint) olive oil

75 g (3 oz) butter

2 garlic cloves, skinned and finely chopped

two 50 g (2 oz) cans anchovy fillets, drained and finely chopped

1 While the asparagus and artichokes are cooling, prepare the remaining vegetables. Cut the cauliflower into florets, discarding any tough stalks.

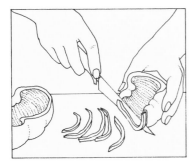

2 Cut the peppers in half lengthways and remove the cores and seeds. Wash the peppers inside and out, dry and cut into strips.

3 Cut the carrots, celery and courgettes into finger-sized sticks. Trim the radishes.

4 Heat the oil and butter in a saucepan until just melted, but not foaming. Add the garlic and cook gently for 2 minutes. Do not allow it to colour.

5 Add the anchovies and cook very gently, stirring all the time, for 10 minutes or until the anchovies dissolve into a paste.

6 To serve. Transfer the dip to an earthenware dish and keep warm over a fondue burner or spirit lamp at the table. Each guest dips the vegetables in the hot anchovy sauce.

DEEP-FRIED MOZZARELLA SANDWICHES
MOZZARELLA IN CARROZZA

0.20	🖻	268 cals

Makes 10

175 g (6 oz) Italian Mozzarella cheese
10 large slices of white bread, crusts removed
salt and freshly ground pepper
2 eggs
175 ml (6 fl oz) milk
75 g (3 oz) plain flour
vegetable oil, for frying

4 Quickly dip each sandwich into the egg mixture, then coat lightly with the flour. Dip again into the egg mixture, shaking off any excess.

5 Pour enough oil into a frying pan to come 1 cm ($\frac{1}{2}$ inch) up the sides of the pan and heat until it is hot.

6 Carefully place the sandwiches in the pan, in a single layer. (If your pan is not large enough you may have to use two pans or cook the sandwiches in batches.) Fry for about 3 minutes on each side until brown. Drain on absorbent kitchen paper and serve immediately.

1 Slice the cheese thinly and arrange on five slices of bread, leaving a narrow margin around the edges. Season with salt and pepper and cover with the remaining bread slices. Cut each sandwich in half diagonally or widthways.

2 Beat the eggs in a shallow bowl and add the milk. Season generously with salt and pepper. Spread flour out on a flat plate.

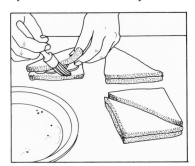

3 Brush a little egg and milk mixture inside edges of sandwiches and press together.

TAGLIATELLE WITH GORGONZOLA SAUCE
TAGLIATELLE CON SALSA AL GORGONZOLA

| 0.25 | 683 cals |

Serves 4

25 g (1 oz) butter
175 g (6 oz) Gorgonzola cheese
150 ml (¼ pint) whipping cream
30 ml (2 tbsp) dry white wine
15 ml (1 tbsp) chopped fresh sage
salt and freshly ground pepper
350 g (12 oz) dried tagliatelle or other long thin pasta

1 Make the sauce. Melt the butter in a heavy-based saucepan.

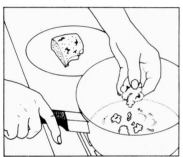

2 Crumble in the Gorgonzola cheese, then stir over gentle heat for 2–3 minutes until melted.

3 Pour in the cream and wine, whisking vigorously. Stir in sage, season and cook, stirring, until sauce thickens. Remove the pan from the heat.

4 Cook the tagliatelle in a large pan of boiling salted water for 8–10 minutes until just tender. Drain thoroughly.

5 Gently reheat the Gorgonzola sauce, whisking vigorously all the time. Taste and adjust seasoning.

6 Divide the tagliatelle equally between four warmed serving bowls. Top each portion with sauce and serve immediately.

PASTA SHELLS WITH CHEESE AND WALNUTS

CONCHIGLIE AL MASCARPONE E NOCI

0.30	644 cals

Serves 4

275 g (10 oz) conchiglie or other
    pasta shapes

salt and freshly ground pepper

25 g (1 oz) butter

225 g (8 oz) Mascarpone or other
    full fat soft cheese

30 ml (2 tbsp) freshly grated
    Parmesan cheese

75 g (3 oz) walnuts, roughly
    chopped

1 Cook the conchiglie in a large pan of boiling salted water for 20 minutes or until just tender. Drain well.

2 In the same pan, melt the butter, add the cheese and stir for about 2–3 minutes until heated through. Do not boil.

3 Add the Parmesan and walnuts, stir, then add the pasta. Mix well until evenly coated with sauce. Season to taste. Serve immediately.

CANNELLONI

| 1.20* | £ | ✳* | 365–487 cals |

* plus extra time to make tomato and
white sauces; freeze before baking at
the end of step 6

Serves 4

30 ml (2 tbsp) olive oil

1 small onion, skinned and very
  finely chopped

1 garlic clove, skinned and crushed

225 g (8 oz) minced veal

100 g (4 oz) chicken livers, roughly
  chopped

225 g (8 oz) frozen chopped
  spinach, thawed

5 ml (1 tsp) chopped fresh basil or
  2.5 ml (½ tsp) dried

2.5 ml (½ tsp) dried oregano

1.25 ml (¼ tsp) grated nutmeg

salt and freshly ground pepper

2 eggs, beaten

50 g (2 oz) Parmesan cheese,
  freshly grated

two 397 g (14 oz) cans chopped
  tomatoes

16 sheets of fresh lasagne (see box)

600 ml (1 pint) white sauce

1 Heat the oil in a heavy-based
frying pan, add the onion and
garlic and fry gently for about
5 minutes until soft and lightly
coloured.

2 Add the minced veal and
chicken livers and fry until
browned, pressing the veal with
the back of a wooden spoon to
break up any lumps.

3 Add the spinach, basil,
oregano, nutmeg and salt and
pepper to taste. Cook, stirring,
until all the liquid has evaporated.
Transfer to a bowl, leave to cool
slightly, then add the eggs and half
of the Parmesan. Stir well to mix.

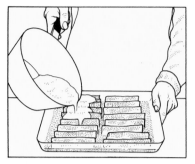

4 Coat the bottom of a large
ovenproof dish with a thin
layer of tomato. Spoon a little of
the veal and spinach filling on one
of the sheets of lasagne. Roll the
lasagne up around the filling, then
place seam side down in the dish.

5 Repeat with the remaining
filling and lasagne until all
used up, arranging the cannelloni
side by side in a single layer.

6 Pour the remaining tomatoes
over the cannelloni, then coat
with the white sauce and sprinkle
with the remaining Parmesan.

7 Bake the cannelloni in the oven
at 190°C (375°F) mark 5 for
30 minutes or until golden brown
and bubbling. Serve hot, straight
from the dish.

CANNELLONI

Fresh lasagne is widely available
at supermarkets as well as Italian
delicatessens. It is good for
making cannelloni because it is
pliable enough to be used
straight from the packet—dried
lasagne has to be boiled and
drained before it can be rolled. If
fresh lasagne is unavailable, it is
quicker to use uncooked dried
cannelloni which can be filled
with a teaspoon or piping bag.

LASAGNE

| 2.10 | £ ✳* | 571–856 cals |

* freeze after step 5

Serves 4–6

30 ml (2 tbsp) olive oil

1 onion, skinned and finely chopped

50 g (2 oz) carrot, peeled and finely chopped

100 g (4 oz) button muchrooms, wiped and sliced

50 g (2 oz) pancetta or unsmoked streaky bacon, rinded and finely diced

1 garlic clove, skinned and crushed

450 g (1 lb) lean minced beef or veal

350 g (12 oz) fresh tomatoes, skinned, seeded and sieved, or 226 g (8 oz) can tomatoes

15 ml (1 tbsp) tomato purée

150 ml ($\frac{1}{4}$ pint) dry white wine

150 ml ($\frac{1}{4}$ pint) beef stock

2 bay leaves

salt and freshly ground pepper

900 ml (1$\frac{1}{2}$ pints) milk

slices of onion, carrot and celery

6 peppercorns

100 g (4 oz) butter

75 g (3 oz) plain flour

12–15 sheets oven-ready lasagne (see box)

50 g (2 oz) freshly grated Parmesan cheese

1 Heat the oil in a large, heavy saucepan, add the onion, carrot, mushrooms, pancetta and crushed garlic. Fry, stirring, for 1–2 minutes. Add the beef or veal and cook over high heat for a further 2 minutes.

2 Stir in the tomatoes and juices, tomato purée, wine, beef stock, 1 bay leaf and seasoning to taste. Bring to the boil, reduce the heat to a simmer, cover and cook for about 35 minutes.

3 Meanwhile, pour the milk into a saucepan, add a few slices of onion, carrot and celery, the peppercorns and remaining bay leaf. Bring slowly to the boil, then remove from heat, cover and leave to infuse for about 15 minutes.

4 Make the béchamel sauce. Strain the infused milk into a jug. Melt the butter in a saucepan, add the flour and cook over low heat, stirring with a wooden spoon, for 2 minutes. Remove the pan from the heat and gradually blend in the milk, stirring after each addition to prevent lumps forming. Bring to the boil slowly and continue to cook for 2–3 minutes, stirring all the time until the sauce thickens. Add seasoning to taste.

5 Brush the inside of a baking dish with butter. Spoon one third of the meat sauce over the base of the dish. Cover this with 4–5 sheets of lasagne and spread over one third of the béchamel. Repeat these layers twice more, finishing with the béchamel sauce which should cover the lasagne completely. Sprinkle grated Parmesan over the top.

6 Stand the dish on a baking sheet. Bake in the oven at 180°C (350°F) mark 4 for about 45 minutes or until the top is well browned and bubbling.

LASAGNE AL FORNO

There are numerous different recipes for lasagne al forno (lasagne baked in the oven): many like this one which combine layers of meat sauce, béchamel and pasta; some with three different cheeses (Parmesan, Mozzarella and Bel Paese) instead of the béchamel, and others with meatballs instead of meat sauce.

This recipe uses oven-ready lasagne, which is easy to use and saves preparation time. It is widely available both at supermarkets and delicatessens and needs no pre-cooking—you simply take it straight from the box and layer it with the béchamel and meat sauces. The same thing can be done with homemade lasagne, which gives a beautiful light result and is well worth making for a dish such as this one which is heavy with other ingredients.

If only the ordinary dried lasagne is available this can of course be used, but you will find it time-consuming and messy, because it has to be boiled in batches before it can be layered with the other ingredients. Always boil it in a very large pan, in *plenty* of boiling salted water (to prevent sticking). Adding 15 ml (1 tbsp) vegetable oil to the water before putting in the lasagne also helps with this problem. Only cook a few sheets at a time (4–6 at the most) to avoid overcrowding the pan, then drain and dry the sheets on a clean tea towel before layering them.

MACARONI PIE
PASTICCIO DI MACCHERONI

| 1.10 | £ | 587 cals |

Serves 6

115 g (4½ oz) butter

30 ml (2 tbsp) olive oil

1 small onion, skinned and finely
chopped

2 garlic cloves, skinned and
crushed

397 g (14 oz) can tomatoes

5 ml (1 tsp) chopped fresh basil
or 2.5 ml (½ tsp) dried, or mixed
herbs

salt and freshly ground pepper

225 g (8 oz) large macaroni

75 g (3 oz) plain flour

568 ml (1 pint) milk

75 g (3 oz) Gruyère cheese, grated

1.25 ml (¼ tsp) freshly grated
nutmeg

60 ml (4 tbsp) freshly grated
Parmesan cheese

45 ml (3 tbsp) dried breadcrumbs

1 Make the tomato sauce. Melt 50 g (2 oz) of the butter in a heavy-based saucepan with the olive oil. Add the onion and garlic and fry gently for 5 minutes until soft but not coloured.

2 Add the tomatoes and their juices with the basil and seasoning to taste, then stir with a wooden spoon to break up the tomatoes. Bring to the boil, then lower the heat and simmer for 10 minutes, stirring occasionally.

3 Meanwhile, plunge the macaroni into a large pan of boiling salted water, bring back to the boil and cook for 10 minutes until just tender.

4 Make the cheese sauce. Melt the remaining butter in a separate saucepan, add the flour and cook over low heat, stirring with a wooden spoon, for about 2 minutes. Remove the pan from the heat and gradually blend in the milk, stirring after each addition to prevent lumps forming. Bring to the boil slowly, stirring all the time until the sauce thickens. Add the Gruyère cheese and seasoning to taste and stir until melted.

5 Drain the macaroni and mix with the tomato sauce. Arrange half of this mixture in a large buttered ovenproof dish.

6 Pour over half of the cheese sauce. Repeat the layers, then sprinkle evenly with the Parmesan and breadcrumbs.

7 Bake the pie in the oven at 190°C (375°F) mark 5 for 15 minutes, then brown under a pre-heated hot grill for 5 minutes. Serve hot.

MUSHROOM AND HAM RISOTTO

RISOTTO ALLA VERONESE

0.50	⊟	f	622 cals

Serves 4

90 g (3½ oz) butter

15 ml (1 tbsp) olive oil

2 small onions, skinned and finely chopped

1 garlic clove, skinned and crushed

225 g (8 oz) mushrooms, wiped and sliced

30 ml (2 tbsp) chopped fresh parsley

150 ml (¼ pint) white wine

900 ml (1½ pints) chicken stock

350 g (12 oz) arborio rice

50 g (2 oz) cooked ham, diced

25 g (1 oz) freshly grated Parmesan cheese

salt and freshly ground pepper

1 Melt 15 g (½ oz) butter and 15 ml (1 tbsp) olive oil in a saucepan. Add half the chopped onion and fry gently for 5 minutes until soft but not coloured.

2 Add the garlic, cook for 1 minute, then add the mushrooms and parsley. Cook gently for 10 minutes until the mushrooms are tender. Stir in 25 g (1 oz) butter and set aside while making the risotto.

3 Bring the stock to the boil in a large saucepan and keep at barely simmering point.

4 In a large, heavy-based saucepan, melt 25 g (1 oz) butter, add the rest of the onion and fry gently for 5 minutes until soft but not coloured.

5 Add the arborio rice and stir well for 2–3 minutes until the rice is well coated with the butter.

6 Add the wine, cook gently, stirring until absorbed. Add 150 ml (¼ pint) of stock as soon as this is absorbed. Continue to add stock in 150 ml (¼ pint) measures, stirring frequently until the risotto is thick and creamy, tender but not sticky. This should take 20–25 minutes. It must not be hurried.

7 Finally, stir in the remaining butter, ham, mushroom mixture and cheese. Taste and adjust seasoning. Serve immediately.

SAFFRON RISOTTO
RISOTTO ALLA MILANESE

0.35	🗄	£	534 cals

Serves 4

1.1 litres (2 pints) beef stock

75 g (3 oz) butter

1 small onion, skinned and finely

350 g (12 oz) arborio rice

pinch of saffron strands

salt and freshly ground pepper

50 g (2 oz) freshly grated Parmesan
  cheese

1 Bring the stock to the boil in a large saucepan and keep at barely simmering point.

2 Meanwhile, in a large, heavy-based saucepan, melt 25 g (1 oz) butter, add the onion and fry gently for 5 minutes until soft but not coloured.

3 Add the arborio rice to the pan and stir well for 2–3 minutes until the rice is well coated with the butter.

4 Add a ladleful of stock to the pan, cook gently, stirring occasionally until the stock is absorbed. Add more stock as soon as each ladleful is absorbed, stirring frequently.

5 When the rice becomes creamy, sprinkle in the saffron with salt and pepper to taste. Continue adding stock and stirring until the risotto is thick and creamy, tender but not sticky. This process should take 20–25 minutes. It must not be hurried.

6 Just before serving, stir in the remaining butter and the Parmesan cheese.

POTATO GNOCCHI
GNOCCHI DI PATATE

| 0.45 | £ ✱* | 586 cals |

* freeze after step 6

Serves 4

900 g (2 lb) old potatoes

salt

50 g (2 oz) butter

1 egg, beaten

225–275 g (8–10 oz) plain flour

150 ml ($\frac{1}{4}$ pint) Pesto, to serve

freshly grated Parmesan cheese,
  to finish

1 Cook the potatoes in their skins in boiling salted water for about 20 minutes until tender. Drain well.

2 Sieve the potatoes while still warm into a large bowl. Add 5 ml (1 tsp) salt, the butter, egg and half the flour. Mix well to bind the potatoes together.

3 Turn out on to a floured surface, gradually adding more flour and kneading until the dough is soft, smooth and slightly sticky.

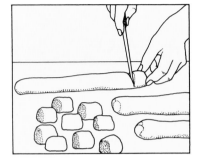

4 With floured hands, roll the dough into 2.5-cm (1-inch) thick ropes. Cut the ropes into 1.5-cm ($\frac{3}{4}$-inch) pieces.

5 Press a finger into each piece to flatten; draw finger towards you to curl sides.

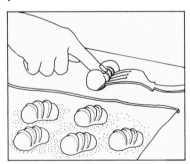

6 Alternatively, you can make a decorative shape by using the same rolling technique, but roll the dumpling over the end of the prongs of a fork. Spread out on a floured tea towel.

7 Bring a large pan of salted water to the boil and reduce to barely simmering. Drop in about twenty-four gnocchi at a time and cook gently for 2–3 minutes or until they float to the surface.

8 With a slotted spoon, remove the gnocchi from the pan, then place them in a buttered serving dish. Cover and keep warm while cooking the remaining gnocchi.

9 When all the gnocchi are cooked, toss them in the Pesto sauce. Serve immediately, sprinkled with freshly grated Parmesan.

GNOCCHI

Gnocchi are little dumplings, in this recipe made from potatoes although there are other versions made with semolina (gnocchi di semolino), and spinach and ricotta cheese (gnocchi verdi). The Italians always eat gnocchi as a first course (primo piatto), sometimes simply sprinkled with melted butter and grated Parmesan cheese, at other times coated in a rich and pungent tomato sauce. The type of gnocchi and the way in which they are served is purely regional; these potato gnocchi are fairly typical of the regions of northern Italy. In Lombardy and Veneto, chopped fresh sage would be added to the melted butter and cheese, whereas in Liguria they like to serve their gnocchi with basil and garlic (pesto) sauce.

FOUR SEASONS PIZZA
PIZZA QUATTRO STAGIONI

1.30* £ ✳* 782 cals

* plus 1½–2 hours rising; freeze after step 6

Makes 4

1 quantity of basic pizza dough (see page 62)

175 g (6 oz) button mushrooms, thinly sliced

45 ml (3 tbsp) olive oil

2 garlic cloves, skinned and crushed

10 ml (2 tsp) chopped fresh basil or 5 ml (1 tsp) dried

two 397 g (14 oz) cans chopped tomatoes

16 slices of Italian salami, rinded

50 g (2 oz) black olives, halved and stoned

8 bottled artichoke hearts, sliced

225 g (8 oz) Italian Mozzarella cheese, thinly sliced

4 tomatoes, skinned and sliced

10 ml (2 tsp) chopped fresh oregano or 5 ml (1 tsp) dried

salt and freshly ground pepper

1 Make the basic pizza dough according to the instructions and leave to rise.

2 Fry the mushrooms lightly in 30 ml (2 tbsp) of the oil with the garlic and basil.

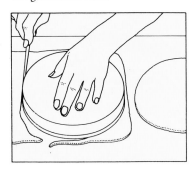

3 Turn the risen dough out on to a floured surface, roll out and cut into four 20-cm (8-inch) circles, using sandwich tins or flan rings as a guide. Make the edges slightly thicker than the centres.

4 Put the circles of dough into oiled sandwich tins. Spread the tomato sauce evenly over dough, right to edges.

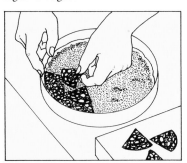

5 Cut each slice of salami into four quarters. Arrange these pieces in one quarter of each pizza, overlapping them to cover tomato sauce. Dot with olives.

6 Arrange the artichokes slices over another pizza quarter, the cheese and tomato over another and mushrooms over the last.

7 Sprinkle the remaining oil over the pizzas with the oregano and seasoning.

8 Leave the pizzas to prove in a warm place for about 30 minutes, then bake in the oven at 220°C (425°F) mark 7 for 25 minutes. Swap over quickly, half-way through the cooking time. Serve hot or cold.

PIZZA WITH FOUR CHEESES
PIZZA QUATTRO FORMAGGI

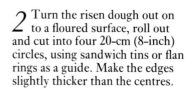

| 1.30* | £ | ✳* | 803 cals |

* plus 1½–2 hours rising; freeze after step 5

Makes 4

1 quantity of basic pizza dough (see page 62)

226 g (8 oz) can tomatoes

salt and freshly ground pepper

100 g (4 oz) Italian Mozzarella cheese, diced

100 g (4 oz) **Bel Paese or Provolone cheese, diced**

100 g (4 oz) **Fontina cheese, diced**

100 g (4 oz) **Taleggio cheese, diced**

20 ml (4 tsp) **olive oil**

20 ml (4 tsp) **chopped fresh mixed herbs or 10 ml (2 tsp) dried**

1 Make the basic pizza dough according to the instructions and leave to rise.

2 Turn the risen dough out on to a floured surface, roll out and cut into four 20-cm (8-inch) circles, using sandwich tins or flan rings as a guide. Make the edges slightly thicker than the centres.

3 Put dough into oiled sandwich tins or flan rings placed on oiled baking sheets.

4 Crush the tomatoes with their juice and spread evenly over the dough, right to the edges. Season to taste.

5 Mix the four cheeses together and sprinkle them evenly over the four pizzas.

6 Sprinkle over the oil and herbs, with salt and pepper to taste. Leave the pizzas to prove in a warm place for about 30 minutes, then bake in the oven at 220°C (425°F) mark 7 for 25 minutes or until the cheeses are melted and the dough is well risen. Swap the oven shelves over half-way through the cooking time. Serve hot or cold.

FARMHOUSE PIZZA
PIZZA CASALINGA

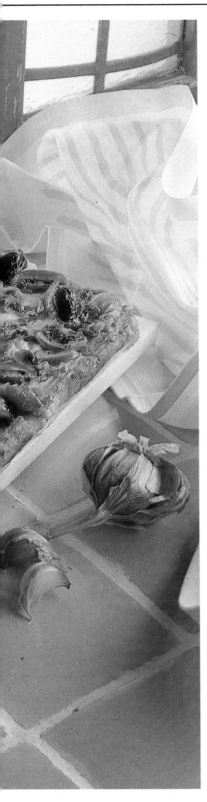

| 1.30 | £ | ✳* | 566 cals |

* plus 1½–2 hours rising; freeze after step 5

Serves 6

1 quantity of basic pizza dough (see page 62)

60 ml (4 tbsp) olive oil

2 garlic cloves, skinned and crushed

225 g (8 oz) mushrooms, wiped

397 g (14 oz) can tomatoes

salt and freshly ground pepper

400 g (14 oz) Italian Mozzarella cheese, thinly sliced

100 g (4 oz) boiled ham, cut into strips

50 g (2 oz) bottled mussels or can anchovy fillets, drained

10 black olives, halved and stoned

20 ml (4 tsp) chopped fresh oregano or 10 ml (2 tsp) dried

1 Make the basic pizza dough according to the instructions and leave to rise.

2 Heat 30 ml (2 tbsp) oil in a heavy-based frying pan. Add the garlic and mushrooms and fry for about 5 minutes until the oil is completely absorbed.

3 Turn the risen dough out on to a floured surface and roll out to a rectangle, approximately 30 × 25 cm (12 × 10 inches). Make the edges slightly thicker than the centre. Put the dough on an oiled baking sheet.

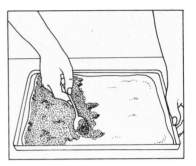

4 Mash the tomatoes with half of their juice so that there are no large lumps, then spread them evenly over the dough, right to the edges. Sprinkle with salt and pepper to taste.

5 Arrange the slices of Mozzarella over the tomatoes, then sprinkle over the strips of ham. Top with the mushrooms and mussels or anchovies, then dot with the olives.

6 Mix together the oregano and remaining oil, and add salt and pepper to taste. Drizzle over the top of the pizza.

7 Leave the pizza to prove in a warm place for about 30 minutes, then bake in the oven at 220°C (425°F) mark 7 for 25 minutes or until the topping is melted and the dough well risen. Cut into serving portions and serve hot or cold.

DEEP-FRIED STUFFED PIZZAS
PANZEROTTI

1.00* £ ✳* 173 cals

* plus 1½–2 hours rising; freeze after step 7

Makes 16

1 quantity of basic pizza dough (see page 62)
397 g (14 oz) can tomatoes
100 g (4 oz) Italian Mozzarella cheese
25 g (1 oz) freshly grated Parmesan cheese
50 g (2 oz) boiled ham, finely diced
salt and freshly ground pepper
vegetable oil, for deep frying

1 Make the basic pizza dough according to the instructions and leave to rise.

2 Cook the tomatoes over high heat, stirring constantly, until reduced to a thick pulp. Leave to cool for about 30 minutes.

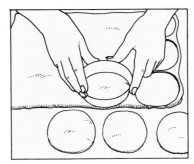

3 Meanwhile, turn the risen dough out on to a floured surface, roll out and cut into sixteen 10-cm (4-inch) circles. Use a plain pastry cutter or the rim of a wine glass or cup as a guide.

4 Spread the cold tomato sauce over the circles of dough, leaving a border at the edge.

5 Roughly chop the Mozzarella. Mix it with Parmesan, ham and seasoning. Sprinkle over one half of dough.

6 Brush the edge of the dough with water, then fold the plain half over the filled half.

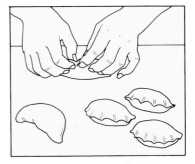

7 Press the edges of the panzerotti together well to seal in the filling, then crimp to make a decorative edge.

8 Heat the oil in a deep-fat frier to 180°C (350°F). Deep-fry the pizzas in batches for 2–3 minutes on both sides until golden. Drain and serve immediately.

MARINATED BEEF *STUFATO ALLA ALTO ATESINA*

3.45* £ £	715–1072 cals

*plus 3–4 days marinating

Serves 4–6

250 ml (9 fl oz) red wine

120 ml (4½ fl oz) red wine vinegar

30 ml (2 tbsp) granulated sugar

2 garlic cloves, skinned and crushed

2 bay leaves

15 ml (1 tbsp) juniper berries, crushed

6 whole cloves

salt and freshly ground pepper

1.6–1.8 kg (3½–4 lb) rolled and tied topside

45 ml (3 tbsp) vegetable oil

60 ml (4 tbsp) raisins

10 ml (2 tsp) plain flour

100 ml (4 fl oz) double cream

chopped fresh parsley, to garnish

1 Pour the red wine, wine vinegar and 300 ml (½ pint) water into a saucepan. Add the sugar, garlic, bay leaves, juniper berries, cloves and 5 ml (1 tsp) salt. Bring slowly to the boil, stirring.

2 Place the beef in an earthenware or glass (not metal) bowl. Pour the hot marinade over the beef, leave until cold, then cover and place in the refrigerator. Leave to marinate for 3–4 days, turning the beef in the marinade twice a day, if possible.

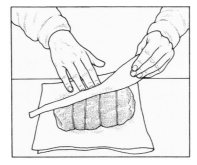

3 When ready to cook, remove the beef from the marinade and pat dry with absorbent kitchen paper. Reserve the marinade.

4 Heat the oil in a heavy flameproof casserole, add the beef and fry quickly on all sides until browned.

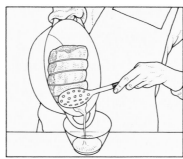

5 Pour off any excess fat, then strain in the reserved marinade. Bring the liquid to the boil, then cover and cook in the oven at 150°C (300°F) mark 2 for 3 hours, or until the beef is very tender when pierced in the centre.

6 Remove the beef from the casserole and place on a carving dish. Set aside to 'rest' in a warm place.

7 Meanwhile, soak the raisins in boiling water for about 10 minutes until plump and juicy. Mix the flour and cream together smoothly. Transfer the casserole to the top of the cooker and gradually stir in the flour and cream mixture. Drain the raisins and add to the sauce, with salt and pepper to taste. Heat gently, stirring constantly, until the sauce thickens. Keep hot.

8 Carve the beef into thin slices and arrange, overlapping, on a warmed serving platter. Drizzle a little of the hot sauce over the meat and sprinkle with the parsley. Pour the remaining sauce into a sauceboat and serve immediately.

MARINATED BEEF

Topside of beef is a popular cut, mainly because the meat is so lean. Many cooks make the mistake of regarding it as a roasting joint, however, and are then disappointed with the end result, which is usually dry, tough and tasteless.

This method of marinating topside in a mixture of red wine and vinegar comes from Germany; the acid in the marinade helps break down the connective tissue in the meat. The longer the meat is left in the marinade the better—it could be safely left in the refrigerator for 1 week, as the wine and vinegar have a preservative effect.

RUMP STEAK IN WHISKY
BISTECCA ALLA WHISKY

| 0.20* | £ £ | 309 cals |

* plus 12 hours marinating

Serves 6

1.1-kg (2½-lb) piece rump steak, about 2 cm (¾ inch) thick

1 small onion, skinned and thinly sliced

2 garlic cloves, skinned

90 ml (6 tbsp) whisky

30 ml (2 tbsp) vegetable oil

freshly ground pepper

salt

watercress sprigs, to garnish

1 Trim off any excess fat from the steak, then place the meat in an edged dish into which it will just fit comfortably.

2 Scatter onion over meat. To make the marinade, crush the garlic and mix with the whisky, oil and pepper. Pour over meat. Cover tightly with cling film and refrigerate for at least 12 hours, turning and basting once.

3 Preheat the grill. Lift the meat out of the marinade and pat the surface dry with absorbent kitchen paper, then place on the rack of the grill pan.

4 Grill the rump steak under a high heat for about 6 minutes each side, depending on how rare you like it.

5 Meanwhile, strain the marinade into a small saucepan and warm gently; adjust seasoning, adding salt at this stage if necessary.

6 Lift the steak on to a serving plate and spoon over the warmed liquid. To serve, garnish the steak with watercress sprigs.

RUMP STEAKS WITH TOMATO, GARLIC AND OLIVE OIL SAUCE   *BISTECCHE ALLA PIZZAIOLA*

| 0.30 | f f | 407 cals |

Serves 4

30 ml (2 tbsp) olive oil, plus extra for frying

2–3 garlic cloves, skinned and sliced

700 g (1½ lb) ripe tomatoes, skinned and roughly chopped, or two 397 g (14 oz) cans tomatoes, drained

15 ml (1 tbsp) chopped fresh oregano or basil, or 5 ml (1 tsp) dried

salt and freshly ground pepper

four 175 g (6 oz) rump steaks, trimmed

100 g (4 oz) large black olives

1 Make the sauce. Heat the oil in a medium saucepan, add the sliced garlic and cook gently for about 1 minute.

2 Add the tomatoes with the herbs and salt and pepper to taste. Boil gently for 15 minutes, until the tomatoes have cooked down but have not completely disintegrated.

3 Heat a little olive oil in a large frying pan. Fry the steaks for 2 minutes on each side.

4 Meanwhile, stone the olives and roughly chop the flesh. Coat steaks with sauce, add olives and cook, covered, for 5 minutes.

ITALIAN-STYLE BRAISED PORK   *ARROSTO DI MAIALE AL LATTE*

2.00	450 cals

Serves 6

15 ml (1 tbsp) vegetable oil

25 g (1 oz) butter

1 kg (2¼ lb) loin of pork, rinded

2 garlic cloves, skinned

1 large onion, skinned and chopped

568 ml (1 pint) milk

5 juniper berries

2 rosemary sprigs, plus extra for garnish

salt and freshly ground pepper

1 Heat the oil and the butter in a large saucepan or flameproof casserole into which the meat will just fit and fry the pork, garlic and onion for about 15 minutes until the pork is browned on all sides. Add the milk, juniper berries, rosemary and seasoning.

2 Bring to the boil, cover, turn the heat down and cook for 1½–2 hours until the pork is tender, turning and basting from time to time.

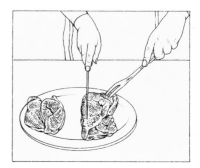

3 Transfer the pork to a warmed serving dish and carve into thick slices. Discard the garlic, juniper berries and rosemary. The milky cooking juices will look curdled, so rub the sauce through a sieve or liquidise in a blender or food processor until smooth. Taste and adjust the seasoning. Pour a little of the sauce over the slices and serve the remaining sauce separately. Garnish with sprigs of rosemary.

ITALIAN-STYLE BRAISED PORK

Cooking pork in milk may seem a very strange combination at first, but it is very popular in Italy. The milk and the long, slow cooking produce the most tender results, making Arrosto di Maiale al Latte, as the Italians call this dish, a firm favourite for Sunday lunches, even with the less tender cuts of pork. The loin used in this recipe is a tender, expensive, cut of pork, but it can be rather dry if roasted in the normal way, because it is so lean. Braising loin of pork in milk ensures that the meat will be moist and succulent, and the flavour of garlic, juniper and rosemary gives the dish a unique aromatic taste.

BRAISED VEAL IN WHITE WINE

OSSO BUCO

| 2.30 | £ | ✳ | 957 cals |

Serves 4

50 g (2 oz) butter

15 ml (1 tbsp) olive oil

1 onion, skinned and finely chopped

4–8 ossi buchi (veal shin, hind cut), sawn into 5 cm (2 inch) lengths, weighing about 1.75 kg (3½ lb)

50 g (2 oz) plain flour

salt and freshly ground pepper

300 ml (½ pint) dry white wine

300 ml (½ pint) veal or chicken stock

finely grated rind of 1 lemon

1 garlic clove, skinned and finely chopped

45 ml (3 tbsp) chopped fresh parsley

Risotto, to serve

1 Melt the butter with the oil in a flameproof casserole, add the onion and fry gently for 5 minutes until soft but not coloured.

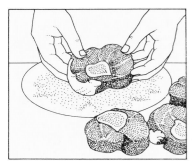

2 Coat the veal in the flour seasoned with salt and pepper. Add to the casserole and fry for about 10 minutes until browned all over.

3 Pour over the wine and boil rapidly for 5 minutes, then add the veal or chicken stock.

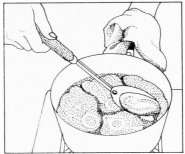

4 Cover the pan tightly and simmer for 1½–2 hours, basting and turning the meat occasionally.

5 When the meat is cooked, transfer to a warmed serving dish, cover and keep warm. If necessary, boil the sauce rapidly to reduce and thicken, then pour over the meat.

6 Mix together the lemon rind, garlic and parsley and sprinkle over the finished dish. Serve hot, with Risotto.

OSSO BUCO

This classic dish is from the city of Milan in Lombardy, where it is always garnished, as here, with lemon rind, garlic and parsley, called gremolata in Italian. Be sure to buy the correct cut of veal—the shin or shank. This contains the marrow, considered to be a great delicacy and traditionally dug out of the bones with a silver spoon.

VEAL ESCALOPES WITH LEMON
SCALOPPINE AL LIMONE

| 0.25 | 305 cals |

Serves 4

4 veal escalopes
30 ml (2 tbsp) plain flour
salt and freshly ground pepper
50 g (2 oz) butter
60 ml (4 tbsp) olive oil
45 ml (3 tbsp) lemon juice
90 ml (6 tbsp) dry white wine
lemon slices and sprigs of Italian
  or continental parsley, to
  garnish

1 Put the escalopes between two sheets of greaseproof paper and bat out until thin with a meat mallet or rolling pin.

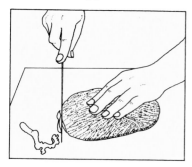

2 Trim the escalopes to size, then coat in the flour seasoned with salt and pepper. Make sure both sides are evenly coated.

3 Melt the butter with the oil in a large, heavy-based frying pan. Add the escalopes and fry for 3–4 minutes on each side until tender. (If you do not have a pan large enough to cook all four escalopes together, either use two frying pans or cook two first and then keep them warm while you are cooking the others.)

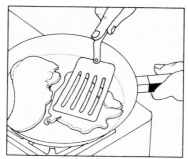

4 During cooking, press the escalopes constantly with a fish slice to help prevent shrinkage and keep them as flat as possible.

5 Transfer the escalopes to a warmed serving platter with a fish slice, cover and keep warm.

6 Add the lemon juice and wine to the pan and stir to combine with the cooking juices. Bubble vigorously for a minute or two, then add salt and pepper to taste. Pour over the escalopes, garnish with lemon slices and parsley sprigs and serve immediately.

ITALIAN FARMHOUSE CHICKEN   *POLLO CACCIATORA*

| 0.50 | £ | ✳ | 458 cals |

Serves 4

25 g (1 oz) butter

30 ml (2 tbsp) olive oil

4 chicken portions

1 medium onion, skinned and chopped

2 garlic cloves, skinned and crushed

225 g (8 oz) button mushrooms, sliced

150 ml ($\frac{1}{4}$ pint) dry white wine

397-g (14-oz) can tomatoes, drained

10 ml (2 tsp) dried mixed herbs

5 ml (1 tsp) dried oregano

salt and freshly ground pepper

1 Melt the butter with the oil in a large flameproof casserole. Add the chicken and fry over moderate heat for 5–10 minutes until well coloured on all sides. Remove from the pan with a slotted spoon and drain on absorbent kitchen paper.

2 Add the onion and garlic to the pan and fry gently until soft. Return the chicken to the pan, add the mushrooms and wine and simmer for 10 minutes.

3 Add the tomatoes, herbs and salt and pepper to taste, then cover and simmer for a further 35 minutes or until the chicken is tender. Taste and adjust seasoning before serving.

CHICKEN WITH PARMA HAM AND CHEESE
POLLO ALLA VALDOSTANA

0.45	£	409 cals

Serves 4

4 boneless chicken breasts, skinned

4 slices of Parma ham or other type of prosciutto

15 ml (1 tbsp) plain flour

5 ml (1 tsp) dried mixed herbs

salt and freshly ground pepper

30 ml (2 tbsp) olive oil

25 g (1 oz) butter

100 g (4 oz) Fontina cheese, grated

150 ml ($\frac{1}{4}$ pint) dry white or rosé wine

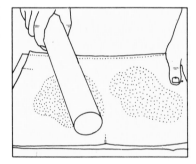

1 Bat the chicken breasts flat with a meat mallet or rolling pin between two sheets of grease-proof paper.

2 Trim the slices of Parma ham to about the same size as the chicken breasts.

3 Put the flour and herbs on a large flat plate, add a liberal sprinkling of salt and pepper and stir well to mix. Coat the chicken pieces on both sides with the flour mixture.

4 Heat the oil with the butter in a large, heavy-based frying pan. Add the chicken pieces and fry over moderate heat for 10 minutes, turning once.

5 Place one slice of ham on top of each chicken breast, then sprinkle the cheese over the top to cover the ham completely.

6 Pour the wine around the chicken and bring to boiling point. Cover the pan tightly, lower the heat to simmering and cook for 5 minutes more until the cheese has melted. Serve hot, with the pan juices poured over the top of the chicken.

CHICKEN WITH ROSEMARY
POLLO AL ROSMARINO

1.00	356 cals

Serves 4

30 ml (2 tbsp) white wine vinegar

7.5 cm (3 inch) sprig of rosemary, chopped

salt and freshly ground pepper

4 chicken leg joints, cut in half

30 ml (2 tbsp) olive oil

lemon wedges, to garnish

1 Put the vinegar into a glass, add 15 ml (1 tbsp) of water, the rosemary and salt and pepper to taste. Stir well, then leave to infuse while cooking the chicken.

2 Season the chicken pieces with salt and pepper. Heat the oil in a large frying pan and, when hot, add the chicken pieces and fry for 5 minutes until they are just golden brown on all sides. Lower the heat and cook uncovered for about 35 minutes.

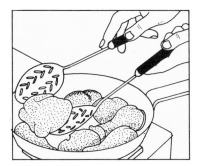

3 Using two slotted spoons, turn the chicken frequently during cooking until the skin is brown and crisp and the juices run clear when flesh is pierced with a fork.

4 Remove the pan from the heat. When the fat has stopped sizzling, pour over the wine vinegar infusion.

5 Return to the heat, boil rapidly to reduce the liquid for about 5 minutes, then serve immediately, garnished with lemon wedges.

ITALIAN FISH STEW   *ZUPPA DI PESCE*

`1.00` 🔲	`481 cals`

Serves 4

good pinch of saffron strands

about 900 g (2 lb) mixed fish fillets
(e.g. red mullet, bream, bass,
brill, monkfish, plaice or cod)

10–12 whole prawns, cooked

60 ml (4 tbsp) olive oil

1 large onion, skinned and finely
chopped

3 garlic cloves, skinned and
crushed

2 slices of drained canned
pimiento, sliced

450 g (1 lb) tomatoes, skinned,
seeded and chopped

2 canned anchovy fillets, drained

150 ml ($\frac{1}{4}$ pint) dry white wine

150 ml ($\frac{1}{4}$ pint) water

2 bay leaves

45 ml (3 tbsp) chopped fresh basil

salt and freshly ground pepper

10–12 mussels, in their shells

4 slices of hot toast, to serve

1 Prepare the saffron water. Soak
the saffron strands in a little
boiling water for 30 minutes.

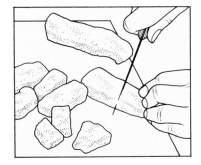

2 Meanwhile, skin the fish and
cut into chunky bite-sized
pieces. Shell the prawns.

3 Heat the oil in a large heavy-
based pan, add the onion, garlic
and pimiento and fry gently for 5
minutes until soft.

4 Add the tomatoes and anchovies and stir with a wooden
spoon to break them up. Pour in
the wine and the water and bring
to the boil, then lower the heat
and add the bay leaves and half
the basil. Simmer uncovered for
20 minutes, stirring occasionally.

5 Add the firm fish to the
tomato mixture, then strain in
the saffron water and add salt and
pepper to taste. Cook for 10 minutes, then add the delicate-
textured fish and cook for a further
5 minutes or until tender.

6 Add the prawns and mussels
and cook, covered, for 5 minutes or until the mussels open.
Remove the bay leaves and discard.

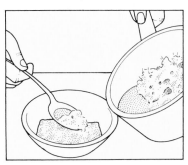

7 To serve, put one slice of toast
in each of four individual soup
bowls. Spoon over the soup,
sprinkle with the remaining basil
and serve at once.

ITALIAN FISH STEW

This type of fish stew is
popular in coastal regions, es-
pecially in the regions around the
Adriatic Sea and in the southern
part of Italy around Sicily.

There are numerous different
versions of fish stew or soup,
called *zuppa di pesce* in Italian,
with recipes varying from one
village and one cook to another —
there are no hard and fast rules.
Burrida is the famous fish and
tomato stew from Genoa; it contains many unusual fish which
are not available outside local
waters, but it can be made
successfully outside the region
with monkfish, octopus and
squid, together with clams,
mussels and shrimps.

Around the Adriatic Sea, fish
soup is called *brodetto* — the
ones from Venice, Rimini and
Ravenna being the most famous.
These fish soups use similar fish
to the Genoese *burrida*, but they
do not contain tomatoes and they
are traditionally served with
bread fried or baked in oil —
called *casada*. Another well-
known Italian fish soup is
caciuccio Livornese, a main course
dish flavoured strongly with
tomatoes and hot red peppers,
and served with *casada*.

Don't worry if you can't find
the authentic fish when making
an Italian fish stew or soup. The
recipe on this page suggests sub-
stitutes which are readily available outside Italy and which will
taste equally good — as long as
you use a good variety and make
sure they are as fresh as possible. Try to include at least some
red or grey mullet; monkfish is
also a good buy — it has a strong
flavour and dense texture, and
does not break up easily during
cooking.

ITALIAN MARINATED TROUT
TROTA AL FINOCCHIO

0.15*	£ £	221 cals

* plus at least 8 hours marinating

Serves 4

---

30 ml (2 tbsp) olive oil

4 whole trout, about 225 g (8 oz)
    each, cleaned

30 ml (2 tbsp) flour

1 small bulb Florence fennel,
    trimmed and finely sliced

1 onion, skinned and finely sliced

300 ml (½ pint) dry white Italian
    wine

finely grated rind and juice of 1
    orange

salt and freshly ground pepper

orange slices and chopped fennel
    tops, to garnish

2 With a sharp knife, score the skin diagonally, being careful not to cut too deeply into the flesh. Set aside.

3 Add the fennel and onion to the frying pan and fry for 5 minutes. Add the wine, orange rind and juice, and seasoning to taste. Bring to the boil. Boil rapidly for 1 minute, add the chopped fennel tops and pour immediately over the fish. Cool.

4 Marinate in the refrigerator for at least 8 hours, but no more than 3 days.

5 Serve at room temperature, garnished with orange slices and the chopped fennel tops.

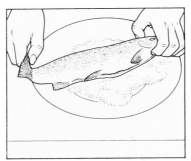

1 Heat the olive oil in a frying pan. Dip the trout in the flour and fry gently for 4 minutes on each side. With a fish slice, transfer the fish to a shallow dish.

ITALIAN MARINATED TROUT

The bulb vegetable Florence fennel looks rather like a squat version of celery with feathery leaves. The flavour of fennel is like aniseed; for the most subtle taste of aniseed, buy white or pale green fennel, for a stronger flavour, choose vegetables which are dark green in colour. In this recipe, fennel is fried with onion and used in a marinade for fish, with which it has a particular affinity. Other more usual uses for fennel are sliced or chopped raw in salads (fennel and tomato are particularly good together), and braised in the oven with stock or a white or cheese sauce. As its name suggests, Florence fennel comes from Italy, where it is used extensively in cooking.

SWEET PEPPER AND TOMATO STEW
PEPERONATA

| 0.45 | £ | ✳ | 156 cals |

Serves 6

75 ml (5 tbsp) olive oil

1 large onion, peeled and finely sliced

6 red peppers, cored, seeded and sliced into strips

2 garlic cloves, skinned and crushed

700 g (1½ lb) ripe tomatoes, skinned and roughly chopped

15 ml (1 tbsp) chopped fresh parsley

salt and freshly ground pepper

1 Heat the oil in a frying pan, add the onion and fry gently for 5 minutes until soft but not coloured.

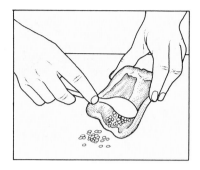

2 Halve the peppers, remove the cores and seeds, then slice the flesh into strips.

3 Add the peppers and garlic, cook gently for 2–3 minutes, then add the tomatoes, parsley and salt and pepper to taste.

4 Cover and cook gently for 30 minutes until the mixture is quite dry: if necessary, remove the lid 10 minutes before the end of cooking and allow the liquid to evaporate. Taste and adjust seasoning before serving either hot or cold.

BAKED TOMATOES WITH ANCHOVIES
POMODORI AL FORNO

0.30	105 cals

Serves 6

3 firm large continental-type
 tomatoes

1.25 ml ($\frac{1}{4}$ tsp) sugar

freshly ground pepper

30 ml (2 tbsp) olive oil

1 small onion, skinned and very
 finely chopped

1–2 garlic cloves, skinned and
 crushed

50 g (2 oz) can anchovy fillets,
 drained and chopped

20 ml (4 tsp) chopped fresh basil or
 10 ml (2 tsp) dried

25 g (1 oz) freshly grated Parmesan
 cheese

fillets of anchovies, to garnish

1 Cut the tomatoes in half cross-ways. Stand them in an oiled baking dish, levelling the bottoms if necessary so that they will stand upright. Sprinkle with the sugar and pepper. Leave to stand.

2 Heat the oil in a heavy-based pan, add the onion and garlic and fry gently for 5 minutes until soft but not coloured.

3 Add the anchovies and cook for a few minutes more, pressing them with a wooden spoon to break them up.

4 Remove from the heat and stir in the basil, with pepper to taste. (Do not add salt because the anchovies are salty enough.)

5 Spoon the mixture on top of the tomato halves, dividing it equally between them, then sprinkle with the Parmesan.

6 Bake the tomatoes in the oven at 220°C (425°F) mark 7 for 10–15 minutes or until just tender and sizzling. Serve hot, garnished with strips of anchovies.

FENNEL AU GRATIN
FINOCCHI GRATINATI

0.40	234–351 cals

Serves 4–6

4 small bulbs of fennel, trimmed

salt and freshly ground pepper

60 ml (4 tbsp) olive oil

60 ml (4 tbsp) butter

50 g (2 oz) Fontina cheese, grated

45 ml (3 tbsp) freshly grated
  Parmesan cheese

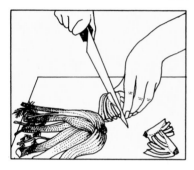

1 Using a sharp knife, carefully cut each bulb of fennel into quarters lengthways.

2 Cook the fennel quarters in a large pan of boiling salted water for 20 minutes until just tender. Drain thoroughly.

3 Heat the oil with the butter in a flameproof gratin dish. Add the fennel and toss to coat in the oil and butter.

4 Turn the fennel quarters cut side up in the dish. Sprinkle with the two cheeses and seasoning.

5 Grill under a preheated hot grill for 5 minutes or until the cheeses are melted and bubbling. Serve hot.

FINOCCHI GRATINATI
The Fontina cheese in this recipe is a hard, mountain cheese with a sweet, nutty flavour. If difficult to obtain, use Gruyère or Emmental instead.

SPINACH WITH SULTANAS AND PINE NUTS
SPINACI ALLA ROMANA

0.30	202 cals

Serves 4

25 g (1 oz) sultanas

900 g (2 lb) washed fresh spinach or
  450 g (1 lb) frozen spinach

25 g (1 oz) butter

30 ml (2 tbsp) olive oil

1 garlic clove, skinned and crushed

25 g (1 oz) pine nuts

salt and freshly ground pepper

1 Put the sultanas in a bowl, pour in enough hot water to cover and leave to soak for 15 minutes until plump.

2 Place the spinach in a saucepan without any water and cook gently for 5–10 minutes, or until thawed if using frozen spinach.

3 Drain the spinach thoroughly and squeeze out as much moisture as possible. Set aside.

4 Melt the butter with the oil in a saucepan, add the garlic and cook gently for 1 minute. Add the spinach and stir until evenly coated with the butter and oil and completely heated through.

5 Drain the sultanas and stir them into the spinach with the pine nuts and salt and pepper to taste. Heat through, then serve immediately to avoid overcooking the spinach.

PANETTONE

1.30* 🔲 🔲	290 cals

* plus rising, proving and cooling
Serves 10

350 g (12 oz) plain white flour

20 g (¾ oz) fresh yeast or 15 g (2¼ tsp) dried

225 ml (8 fl oz) tepid milk

100 g (4 oz) butter, softened

3 egg yolks

50 g (2 oz) caster sugar

75 g (3 oz) candied peel, chopped

50 g (2 oz) sultanas

pinch of grated nutmeg

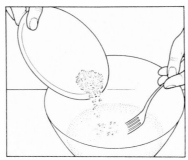

1 Prepare the dough. Sift the flour into a large bowl and make a well in the centre. Blend the fresh yeast with the milk. If using dried yeast, sprinkle it into the milk and leave in a warm place for 15 minutes until frothy. Add the yeast liquid to the flour and mix well together, gradually drawing in the flour from the sides of the bowl. Leave to stand in a warm place for 45 minutes or until doubled in bulk.

2 Add the softened butter to the dough with 2 of the egg yolks, the sugar, candied peel, sultanas and nutmeg. Mix well together. Leave to stand again in a warm place for a further 45 minutes or until doubled in bulk.

3 Meanwhile, cut 3 strips of baking parchment, each one measuring 56 × 25.5 cm (22 × 10 inches). Fold each piece over lengthways.

4 Stand the 3 pieces of parchment together on a greased baking sheet to make a 17 cm (6½ inch) circle and secure with staples. Place the dough inside the paper and leave in a warm place for about 1 hour or until risen to the top of the paper.

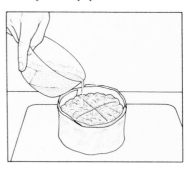

5 Cut the top of the dough in the shape of a cross, then pour over the last egg yolk. Bake on the lowest shelf of the oven at 200°C (400°F) mark 6 for 20 minutes, then lower the temperature to 180°C (350°F) mark 4 for a further 40 minutes or until a skewer inserted in the centre comes out clean. Leave to cool in the paper, then store in an airtight tin for a maximum of 1 week.

PANETTONE

Panettone comes from Milan in northern Italy. The cakes are exported in attractive tall boxes, which can be seen hanging in Italian delicatessens all over the world. Panettone made at home is not so tall as the commercial varieties, and its texture is not quite so open, but it makes a deliciously light alternative to heavy Christmas fruit cakes.

GENOESE APPLE CAKE
TORTA DI MELA

1.30* ⊟ ✳* 456 cals

* plus 2–3 hours cooling time; freeze after cooling in step 9

Serves 6

4 eggs

150 g (5 oz) caster sugar

150 g (5 oz) plain flour

5 ml (1 tsp) baking powder

pinch of salt

100 g (4 oz) butter, melted and cooled

90 ml (6 tbsp) milk

finely grated rind of 1 lemon

700 g (1½ lb) Golden Delicious apples, peeled, cored and thinly sliced

5–10 ml (1–2 tbsp) vegetable oil

15–30 ml (1–2 tbsp) dried breadcrumbs

icing sugar, to finish

1 Put the eggs and sugar in a heatproof bowl standing over a pan of gently simmering water.

2 Whisk for 10–15 minutes until the mixture is thick and pale and holds a ribbon trail when the beaters are lifted. (Alternatively, if you have a table top electric mixer, this can be used instead of whisking over hot water.)

3 Remove the bowl from the heat and continue whisking until the mixture is cool.

4 Sift the flour with the baking powder and salt. Fold half of this mixture gently into the whisked eggs and sugar.

5 Slowly trickle the melted butter around the edge of the bowl and fold it in gently. Take care not to stir too heavily or the mixture will lose air.

6 Fold in the remaining flour mixture, then the milk and lemon rind. Fold in the apples.

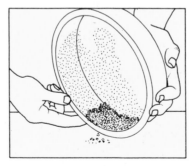

7 Brush the inside of a 23-cm (9-inch) diameter cake tin with oil. Sprinkle with breadcrumbs, then shake off the excess.

8 Pour the cake mixture into the tin and bake in the oven at 180°C (350°F) mark 4 for about 40 minutes until a skewer inserted in the centre comes out clean.

9 Leave the cake to rest in the tin for about 5 minutes, then turn out on to a wire rack and leave for 2–3 hours to cool completely. Sift icing sugar over the top of the cake just before serving.

TORTA DI MELE

This recipe for a Genoese sponge, which is heavy with sweet dessert apples, is made in the classic way by whisking together eggs and sugar over heat until thick and mousse-like, then folding in sifted flour and finally trickling in melted butter. This method gives a light, airy result typical of any whisked or Genoese sponge. If you are in a hurry, you can cut corners with this particular recipe, because the weight of the apples tends to disguise the texture of the cake! Simply beat the eggs and sugar together with a wooden spoon, then fold in the flour mixture, followed by the melted butter, milk, lemon rind and apples.

CHOCOLATE 'SALAMI'
SALAME AL CIOCCOLATO

1.00*	🯄 £ £ ✳*	472–629 cals

* plus 1 hour firming up and about 4 hours freezing; freeze at the end of step 6

Serves 6–8

50 g (2 oz) split blanched almonds

20 Petit Beurre biscuits

225 g (8 oz) plain chocolate, broken into small pieces

175 g (6 oz) unsalted butter, cut into small pieces

45 ml (3 tbsp) almond-flavoured liqueur or brandy

1 egg yolk

25 g (1 oz) ground almonds

1 Spread the blanched almonds out evenly in a grill pan and toast under a moderate grill for a few minutes until evenly browned. Shake the pan frequently so that the almonds do not burn.

2 Transfer the nuts to a nut grinder or food processor and work until finely ground.

3 Put the biscuits in a heavy bowl and crush roughly with the end of a rolling pin. Take out a handful of the crushed biscuits and set aside.

4 Put the chocolate pieces, butter and liqueur in a large heatproof bowl standing over a pan of gently simmering water. Heat gently until melted, stirring occasionally to combine the ingredients.

5 Pour the melted chocolate mixture into the bowl of crushed biscuits. Add the toasted nuts and egg yolk and mix well to combine. Leave in a cool place for about 1 hour to firm up.

6 Turn the mixture out on to a large sheet of lightly buttered foil. With a palette knife and your hands, shape into a sausage about 23 cm (9 inches) long, with tapering ends. Wrap in the foil and freeze for about 4 hours or until the mixture is solid.

7 Crush the reserved biscuits very finely to a powder in an electric blender or food processor, then mix with the ground almonds.

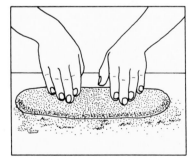

8 Unwrap the 'salami' and roll in the powder until evenly coated. Leave to stand for 1 hour before serving.

RICOTTA CHEESECAKE
BUDINO DI RICOTTA

| 1.00* | £ £ | ✳* | 452 cals |

* plus 2–3 hours cooling; freeze after step 5

Serves 4

350 g (12 oz) Ricotta or curd cheese

3 egg yolks, beaten

100 g (4 oz) sugar

50 ml (2 fl oz) rum or brandy

50 g (2 oz) ground almonds

40 g (1½ oz) chopped candied peel

grated rind of 1 lemon

caster sugar, to decorate

1 Grease and flour a 20.5-cm (8-inch) cake tin and set aside until required.

2 Push the Ricotta or curd cheese through a sieve into a bowl, beat in the egg yolks and sugar.

3 Add the rum, beat well, then fold in the ground almonds, candied peel and lemon rind.

4 Pour into the prepared tin and bake in the oven at 180°C (350°F) mark 4 for 30–40 minutes or until firm and slightly shrunken from the sides of the tin.

5 Open the door of the oven and switch off. Leave the cheesecake inside the oven for about 2–3 hours to cool with the door ajar.

6 To serve. Carefully remove the cheesecake from the tin and dredge with caster sugar.

DEEP-FRIED PASTRY TWISTS

CENCI

0.45	🍴	£	43 cals

Makes 50

300 g (11 oz) plain flour

2 eggs, beaten

45 ml (3 tbsp) rum

60 ml (4 tbsp) caster sugar

5 ml (1 tsp) baking powder

pinch of salt

vegetable oil, for deep frying

icing or caster sugar, for sprinkling

1 Make the dough. Sift 250 g (9 oz) of the flour into a bowl. Make a well in the centre and add the next five ingredients.

2 Mix the ingredients well together with a fork until they come together as a dough.

3 Sprinkle the work surface with some of the remaining flour. Turn the dough out on to the floured surface and gather into a ball with your fingers. Knead until smooth.

4 Cut the dough into quarters. Roll out one quarter of the dough until almost paper thin, adding more flour to the work surface as necessary.

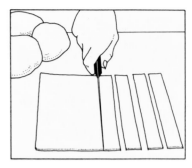

5 Cut into strips about 15 cm (6 inches) long and 2.5 cm (1 inch) wide.

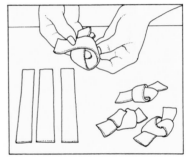

6 Tie the strips into loose knots. Repeat rolling, cutting and tying with the remaining three quarters of dough.

7 Heat the oil in a deep-fat frier to 190°C (375°F). Add 4–5 of the pastry twists to the oil and deep-fry for 1–2 minutes until golden. Drain on absorbent paper while frying the remainder. Sift icing sugar over the twists while they are hot. Serve warm or cold.

ORANGE WATER ICE
GRANITA ALL'ARANCIA

| 0.25* | £ | ✳ | 161 cals |

* plus 8 hours freezing

Serves 6

175 g (6 oz) sugar

450 ml (¾ pint) water

10 large oranges

1½ lemons

1 Make the sugar syrup. Place the sugar and water in a medium saucepan. Heat gently until the sugar dissolves, then boil gently for 10 minutes without stirring.

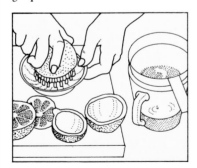

2 Meanwhile, using a potato peeler, thinly pare off the rind from four of the oranges and the lemons.

3 Add the orange and lemon rind to the sugar syrup and leave to go quite cold.

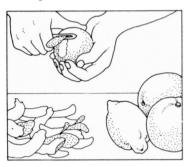

4 Squeeze the juice from the four oranges and the lemons. Strain into a measuring jug — there should be 450 ml (¾ pint).

5 Strain the cold syrup into a shallow freezer container and stir in the fruit juices. Mix well, cover and freeze for about 4 hours until mushy in texture.

6 Remove from the freezer and turn the frozen mixture into a bowl. Beat well with a fork to break down the ice crystals. Return to the freezer container and freeze for at least 4 hours until the mixture is firm.

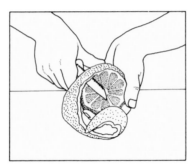

7 Meanwhile, using a serrated knife, cut away the peel and pith from the remaining oranges.

8 Slice the oranges down into thin rings, ease out and discard any pips. Place the oranges in a serving bowl; cover tightly with cling film and refrigerate until serving time.

9 Place the water ice in the refrigerator for 45 minutes to soften before serving. Serve with the fresh orange slices.

--- VARIATIONS ---

Lemon Water Ice
Granita al Limone
With 6–8 lemons as a basis, follow the recipe using the pared rind of four lemons and enough juice to give 450 ml (¾ pint).

Strawberry Water Ice
Granita di Fragole
With 700 g (1½ lb) strawberries, puréed and sieved, and the pared rind and juice of 1 orange as a basis, follow the recipe, using the strawberry purée and orange juice instead of the orange and lemon juices in step 4.

Coffee Water Ice
Granita di Caffè
Put 30 ml (2 tbsp) sugar and 50 g (2 oz) finely ground Italian coffee in a jug, pour over 600 ml (1 pint) boiling water and leave to stand for 1 hour. Strain the coffee through a filter paper or muslin, then follow the recipe after the straining in step 5.

ZABAGLIONE

| 0.15 | 🍴 | 169 cals |

Serves 6

4 egg yolks

65 g (2½ oz) caster sugar

100 ml (4 fl oz) Marsala

sponge fingers, to serve

1 Put the egg yolks and sugar in a large heatproof bowl. Beat together, then add the Marsala and beat until mixed.

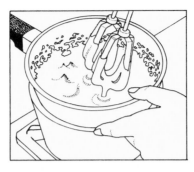

2 Place the bowl over a saucepan of simmering water and heat gently, whisking the mixture until it is very thick and creamy.

3 To serve. Pour the zabaglione into six glasses and serve immediately, with sponge fingers.

FRESH PEACH ICE CREAM *GELATO ALLA PESCA*

0.15* £ ✳ 208 cals

* plus 5–6 hours freezing and 30
minutes standing before serving

Serves 6

350 ml (12 oz) fresh ripe peaches
300 ml (½ pint) condensed milk
grated rind and juice of 1 lemon
300 ml (10 fl oz) whipping cream
peach slices and fan wafers, to
   decorate (optional)

1 Using a sharp knife, quarter
the peaches and remove the
skins, discarding the stones.

2 Roughly slice the peaches into
a blender or food processor,
add the milk, lemon rind and juice
and the cream. Blend well until
the mixture is quite smooth.

3 Pour the mixture out into ice-
cube trays (without divisions)
or a shallow freezer container,
freeze for about 2 hours until
mushy in texture.

4 Turn into a large, chilled basin
and mash with a fork. Return
to the freezer for 3–4 hours to be-
come firm.

5 About 30 minutes before
serving, remove from the
freezer and leave the ice cream to
soften at room temperature. Serve
decorated with peach slices and a
fan wafer, if wished.

FLORENTINE TIPSY CAKE
ZUCOTTO

0.45* £ £ ✳ 902 cals

* plus 12 hours chilling

Serves 6

50 g (2 oz) blanched almonds

50 g (2 oz) hazelnuts

45 ml (3 tbsp) brandy

30 ml (2 tbsp) orange-flavoured liqueur

30 ml (2 tbsp) cherry- or almond-flavoured liqueur

350 g (12 oz) trifle sponges or Madeira cake

150 g (5 oz) plain chocolate

450 ml (15 fl oz) double cream

150 g (5 oz) icing sugar

25 g (1 oz) cocoa powder, to decorate

1 Spread the almonds and hazelnuts out separately on a baking tray and toast in the oven at 200°C (400°F) mark 6 for 5 minutes until golden.

2 Transfer the hazelnuts to a clean tea towel and rub off the skins while still warm. Spread all the nuts out to cool for 5 minutes and then roughly chop.

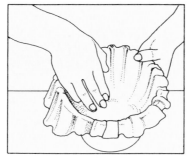

3 Line a 1.4-litre (2½-pint) pudding basin or round-bottomed bowl with damp muslin.

4 In a separate bowl, mix together the brandy and the liqueurs and set aside.

5 Split the trifle sponges in half through the middle (if using Madeira cake, cut into 1 cm (½ inch) slices). Sprinkle with the brandy and liqueurs.

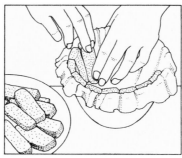

6 Line the basin with the moistened split sponges, reserving enough to cover the top.

7 Using a sharp knife, chop 75 g (3 oz) of the plain chocolate into small pieces, and set aside.

8 In a separate bowl, whip the cream with 125 g (4 oz) icing sugar until stiff and fold in the chopped chocolate and nuts.

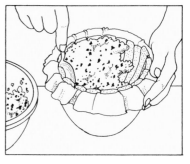

9 Divide this mixture in two and use one half to spread over the sponge lining in an even layer.

10 Melt the remaining chocolate, cool slightly, then fold into the remaining cream mixture. Use this to fill the centre of the pudding.

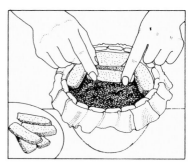

11 Level the top of the zuccotto and cover with the remaining moistened sponge. Trim edges. Cover and refrigerate for at least 12 hours.

12 To serve. Uncover, invert a flat serving plate over basin and turn upside down. Lift off the bowl, and carefully remove the muslin. Serve cold, dusted with the remaining icing sugar and cocoa powder.

BASIC PIZZA DOUGH

45 ml (3 tbsp) lukewarm milk
20 g ($\frac{3}{4}$ oz) fresh yeast
3.75 ml ($\frac{3}{4}$ tsp) sugar
300 g (11 oz) strong white bread flour
7.5 ml ($1\frac{1}{2}$ tsp) salt
30 ml (2 tbsp) olive oil
about 90 ml (6 tbsp) lukewarm water

1 Put the milk in a warmed jug and crumble in the yeast with your fingers. Add the sugar and stir to dissolve, then stir in 4 tbsp of the flour.

2 Cover the jug with a clean tea towel and leave in a warm place for about 30 minutes or until frothy.

3 Sift the remaining flour and the salt into a warmed large bowl. Mix in the yeast with a fork, then add the oil and enough water to draw the mixture together.

4 Turn the dough out on to a floured surface and knead for 10 minutes until it is smooth and elastic.

5 Put the ball of dough in a large floured bowl, cover with a clean tea towel and leave in a warm place for $1\frac{1}{2}$–2 hours until doubled in bulk.

INDEX

Anchovy:
  Baked tomatoes with
    anchovies 45
  Hot anchovy dip 10
Apple:
  Genoese apple cake 51

Beef:
  Lasagne 16
  Marinated beef 31
  Rump steak in whisky 32
  Rump steaks with tomato, garlic
    and olive sauce 33

Cakes:
  Florentine tipsy cake 60
  Genoese apple cake 51
  Panettone 49
Cannelloni 14
Cheese. *See also* Gorgonzola,
  Mozzarella and Ricotta
  Chicken with Parma ham and
    cheese 38
  Pasta shells with cheese and
    walnuts 13
  Pizza with four cheeses 25
Cheesecake:
  Ricotta cheesecake 54
Chicken:
  Chicken with Parma ham and
    cheese 38
  Chicken with rosemary 39
  Italian farmhouse chicken 37
Chocolate 'salami' 52
Coffee water ice 56

Deep-fried pastry twists 55
Deep-fried mozzarella
  sandwiches 11
Deep-fried stuffed pizzas 29
Desserts 54–61

Farmhouse pizza 27

Fennel au gratin 46
Figs, Parma ham with 4
Fish stew, Italian 41
Florentine tipsy cake 60
Four seasons pizza 24

Genoese apple cake 51
Gnocchi (potato) 23
Gorgonzola sauce, tagliatelle
  with 12

Italian farmhouse chicken 37
Italian fish stew 41
Italian marinated trout 43
Italian-style braised pork 34

Lasagne 16
Lemon water ice 56

Macaroni pie 19
Marinated beef 31
Marinated mushroom salad 5
Melon, Parma ham with 4
Mozzarella:
  Deep-fried mozzarella
    sandwiches 11
  Mozzarella-stuffed tomatoes 7
Mushroom:
  Marinated mushroom salad 5
  Mushroom and ham risotto 20

Orange water ice 56
Osso buco 35

Panettone 49
Parma ham:
  Chicken with Parma ham and
    cheese 38
  Parma ham with melon or
    figs 4
Pasta shells with cheese and
  walnuts 13
Pastry twists, deep-fried 55
Peach:
  Fresh peach ice cream 59
Pine nuts, spinach with sultanas
  and 46

Pizza:
  Deep-fried stuffed pizzas 29
  Farmhouse pizza 27
  Four seasons pizza 24
  Pizza with four cheeses 25
Pork:
  Italian-style braised pork 34
Potato gnocchi 23

Ricotta cheesecake 54
Risotto:
  Mushroom and ham risotto 20
  Saffron risotto 21
Rosemary, chicken with 39
Rump steak in whisky 32
Rump steaks with tomato, garlic and
  olive sauce 33

Saffron risotto 21
Seafood salad 8
Spinach with sultanas and pine
  nuts 46
Starters 4–11
Strawberry water ice 56
Sweet pepper and tomato stew 44

Tagliatelle with Gorgonzola sauce 12
Tomato:
  Baked tomatoes with
    anchovies 45
  Mozzarella-stuffed tomatoes 7
  Rump steaks with tomato, garlic
    and olive sauce 33
  Sweet pepper and tomato stew 44
Trout:
  Italian marinated trout 43

Veal:
  Lasagne 16
  Osso buco 35
  Veal escalopes with lemon 36

Walnut:
  Pasta shells with cheese and
    walnuts 13
Water ices 56

Zabaglione 58

Published by Ebury Press
Division of The National Magazine Company Ltd
Colquhoun House
27–37 Broadwick Street
London W1V 1FR

The Good Housekeeping Institute is the food and consumer research centre of
Good Housekeeping magazine.

Printed and bound in Italy by New Interlitho, S.p.a., Milan